THE ENCHANTED HILL

THE STORY OF HEARST CASTLE AT SAN SIMEON

BY CARLETON M. WINSLOW, JR.
& NICKOLA L. FRYE

With a Special Supplement by
TAYLOR COFFMAN,
SENIOR GUIDE, HEARST CASTLE

Published Exclusively for
OGDEN FOOD SERVICE CORPORATION

By Rosebud Books
Los Angeles

Contents

 Rosebud Books
5900 Wilshire Boulevard
Los Angeles, California 90036

Cover and book design by Laura LiPuma
Cover photograph by Jeff Hosier and Jim Englund
Plot drawing of the Castle and grounds by William S. Kerr

Printed in Japan
ISBN 0-86558-003-0

Acknowledgements

The publisher is deeply indebted to several individuals for the remarkable illustrations in *The Enchanted Hill*, among them: Ken Raveill, Baron Wolman, Jeff Hosier and Jim Englund with the assistance of Jerry Grimm, Alan Mims, and Rick H. Smith, Ronald Whaley, John White, Mrs. Mable Souza, and Diana Peterson. Many of the historical photographs are from the collection of Carleton M. Winslow which is presently catalogued at the California Polytechnic State University, San Luis Obispo, California 93401.

Second Printing May 1981
Third Printing April 1982

Largest and most imposing of San Simeon's rooms, the Assembly Room is a treasure house of architectural objects as well as decorative and fine arts.

Chapter One

THE ENCHANTED HILL: AN INTRODUCTION

Over half a century ago a man named William Randolph Hearst began to fulfill a dream. He had inherited property from his mother and father which included fifty miles of shoreline on a remote stretch of the Pacific Coast, halfway between San Francisco and Los Angeles, and encompassed over two hundred and fifty thousand acres of land. The total area was approximately one-half the size of the state of Rhode Island. The future site of the Castle was sixteen hundred feet above the sea, and on a clear day Mr. Hearst could look west across the sparkling Pacific Ocean toward the Orient. But it was more satisfying to look north and east for the most distant blue mountains belonged to him. He called the spot La Cuesta Encantada — The Enchanted Hill.

Today William Randolph Hearst, his wife Millicent, his close friend Marion Davies, his architect Julia Morgan, and the host of friends, acquaintances, and associates who haunted the Castle have vanished from the Enchanted Hill, but the structures which they built and enjoyed remain enlivened by nearly a million visitors each year. The visitors are drawn to the Castle by the view, the gardens, the buildings, and the Collection, but most of all they are drawn by the mystique that permeates the name of Hearst Castle.

Visitors to the Castle are full of questions. What style is it? How many books are there in the library? How much did it cost to build? How many people worked there in its heyday? Why was it left unfinished? The key question to be asked is,

A perfect symmetry; the quiescent Indoor Swimming Pool.

At once imposing and picturesque, 100 room La Casa Grande reaches skyward from the Main Terrace.

What *is* Hearst Castle? Each person will conclude his or her own answer, but we would like to offer some suggestions culled from years of observation and bountiful suggestions.

Hearst Castle is a group of buildings which function as a villa or country house, in the shape of an Italian hill town, which we know is usually dominated by a cathedral or monastery. In no sense of the word is Mr. Hearst's edifice a ''castle''. That word implies defense, and although it did protect the owner from the curious, it lacks the architectural features generally associated with castles.

Some have regarded it as a rich man's plaything, the largest toy in the world. And, indeed, Mr. Hearst appears to have taken an almost childlike delight in the enterprise. He was anxious for others to enjoy his plaything as well. In a letter to his architect, Julia Morgan, on October 18, 1927, he says:

Miss Julia Morgan
Merchant Exchange Building
San Francisco, California

Dear Miss Morgan:
   I am leaving for the East tomorrow, Wednesday night. I have a few last words, as it were, to say about the Hill.
   I think we must positively proceed immediately to build certain animal houses and shelters. I thought at one time that it was desirable to hide the houses in places where they would not be particularly conspicuous, but I find that the animals collect around such feeding places and shelters in distant spots, and we would have our animals where we would never see them.
   I would suggest, therefore, that we make these shelters exceedingly picturesque log houses and put them in certain picturesque locations not far from the main road. There are a number of tree clumps along the road where such shelters could be picturesquely located.
   Will you kindly have these locations picked out at your earliest convenience?
   I think the giraffes should be transferred from where they are. Nobody yet who has come to the ranch has seen the giraffes.
   If you want to consult me about the locations, I suggest that you make the locations and then send me a road map with the locations marked on it, and perhaps some photographs and sketches of what it is proposed to do . . .

Sincerely,
W.R. Hearst

Clearly, his purpose in collecting paintings, sculptures, and giraffes was to delight his friends.

In addition to the *Expanded Toy Box Theory* to explain Mr. Hearst's motivation, we list the following:

The Expanded Camp Theory. The Hill and its buildings can be considered a camp made permanent. La Casa Grande is the great communal tent and the guest houses are the sleeping tents clustered around. This idea is reinforced by the fact that the hill was originally a campsite and that the use of catsup, A-1 sauce and mustard jars, which so delight the visitor, seems consistent with that idea.

Italian cypresses and palms near the North Terrace.

William Randolph Hearst with his favorite dachshund, Helen.

The Warehouse Museum Theory. That the buildings were designed to contain one of the largest personal art collections in the world can hardly be disputed. The size and shape of many rooms were dictated more by the characteristics of the contents, such as the tapestries, than by the habitability of the rooms.

The Corporate Headquarters Theory. The Enchanted Hill certainly was a corporate headquarters for all of the Hearst corporations and subsidiaries in the sense that it was contained in the person of Mr. Hearst himself, just as Charlemagne, the early King of the Franks, had no fixed capitol and moved most of the Court of the Holy Roman Empire with him. However, except for the Gothic Study and the offices to the east of it, there are few hallmarks of international corporate business. There are no files and no business machines — just a board-room and a multiplicity of telephones.

The Resort Hotel Theory. The Enchanted Hill is sometimes perceived as a motel in lavish scale, a sort of celestial Boca Raton where everything is free, except the telephone bill.

The Phoebe Apperson Hearst Memorial Building Theory. Mr. Hearst's mother died just before the planning and construction of the Castle had begun. As an only child, Mr. Hearst had been much closer to his mother than to his father or to anybody else in the family. While he did not always conduct his private affairs as his mother would have wished, and she did not hesitate in letting him know her disapproval, he still had the highest regard for her.

With such widely differing definitions of the nature and function of the Castle, it is understandable that this group of buildings should appeal to people of many interests beyond art and architecture. There are elements of uniqueness in its construction engineering; ornamental horticulture; furniture design; motion picture personalities; restoration and rehabilitation; social history of the 1920s and 1930s; journalism; Indian and early Spanish colonial history; wrought iron; ceramics; Spanish history; oriental rugs; Persian tile and pottery; Greek pottery; silver; San Luis Obispo County history; botany; Greek and Roman history and mythology; tapestries; and zoology.

Clearly, no one need feel left out because he or she is not an art historian. So diversified are the areas of interest touched on by the Enchanted Hill that no one book, short of an encyclopedia, can address them all.

The rich history that lies behind the land, the people, the gardens, the architecture, and the Collection contains some measure of controversy and mystery, and if these two qualities are used as crude standards, surely Hearst Castle must rank as one of the most intriguing buildings in Western civilization.

A harmony of light, space, and form makes the Neptune Pool *the* architectural gem of the Enchanted Hill.

Below the Castle the grassy hills of the Hearst Ranch slope gently to the coastal plain. Cattle have grazed this land since the early mission days.

Chapter Two

GEORGE HEARST AND PHOEBE APPERSON HEARST

The central coast of California upon which William Randolph Hearst built his ranch has a long and varied history. It was first hunted in prehistoric times by the Salinan Indians, who occupied these rugged areas of the south-central coast.

In 1769, Juan Gaspar de Portolá led a Spanish expedition through the Salinan territory. Two years later, in July 1771, Mission San Antonio de Padua, founded by the Franciscan order, became the first mission to be established in this area. Mission San Miguel Archangel was founded in July of 1797, in the southern Salinan area.

Rancho San Simeon, which belonged to the missions, was secularized in 1836, and divided into three great ranchos: San Simeon, which consisted of 4,468 acres; Santa Rosa with 13,183 acres; and Piedra Blanca, the largest with 49,000 acres.

By 1852, a whaling station had been established at San Simeon Point on the land adjacent to the natural bay of San Simeon. The whalers practiced shore whaling. Small boats went out and intercepted the migrating whales. The dead whales were towed to shore and cut up and hoisted onto the wharf, where the oil was rendered in huge trypots. Artifacts connected with whaling are on display at Sebastian's Store in the village of San Simeon.

George Hearst, the father of William Randolph Hearst, was born in Missouri in 1820, the son of William and Elizabeth Hearst. Because of the isolation of the farm and the need for his labor, George Hearst found it difficult as a child to attend

The abrupt projection of San Simeon Point provides one of the the very few safe anchorages along a rugged stretch of California coastline.

The original ranch house of 1878, built by Senator Hearst and still in use today.

The Mission warehouse today.

school. He learned to read and write, but his practical education involved learning about the earth from neighboring miners, and geology and mineralogy from books borrowed from Dr. Silas Reed, a neighbor.

In the spring of 1850, George Hearst followed the lure of gold to California. He was better equipped to succeed at wrenching a living from the earth than many others seeking gold. He crossed the continent by horse and was fully prepared to face the hardships of making his fortune by mining.

After ten lean years in the mines in California, Hearst and two partners, Melville Atwood and A.E. Head, struck it rich. Near Virginia City, Nevada, they had purchased a half interest in a claim. Their mine, which proved to contain no gold, was part of the Comstock Lode and assayed rich in silver.

In 1860, George Hearst, learning that his mother was ill, returned to Missouri. After her death, his thoughts turned to Phoebe Apperson, the daughter of a Missouri neighbor.

Phoebe Elizabeth Apperson was born in Missouri into an old Virginia family on December 3, 1842. Her parents, Randolph and Drusilla, were prosperous slave owners with a large farm on the Meramec River. They occupied a social position of some standing in their community. Phoebe was a tiny woman with Dresden doll features. She spoke precise English and had learned French, an unusual achievement in rural Missouri.

But the courtship of George Hearst and Phoebe was complicated. He was forty years old and uncouth in both appearance and manner. He drank, chewed tobacco and swore. He was hardly the epitome of a proper suitor for eighteen-year-old Phoebe.

To Phoebe, George Hearst represented exotic lands, adventure and romance. In the bargain he was a handsome man. Her parents objected to the union and caused a year's delay in the matrimonial plans.

Miss Apperson took the situation into her own hands when she and George Hearst eloped. They were married in Stedman, Missouri on June 15, 1862. The newlyweds took the luxury route to California in October of the same year. They traveled by train to New York, by boat to Panama, across the isthmus, and then boarded another vessel to San Francisco. The pregnant Phoebe was in great discomfort on the Pacific leg of their journey. On board ship were Mr. and Mrs. David Peck and their two-year-old son Orrin, who would later paint the portrait of William Randolph Hearst which hangs in the Gothic Study. The families remained friends all their lives.

In 1865, George Hearst purchased the Piedra Blanca Rancho for thirty thousand dollars. He improved the port of San Simeon, and built a new wharf in 1878. He later bought the Santa Rosa Rancho, and used all three parcels of land for raising

One of the great empire-builders of nineteenth century America, George Hearst.

An early photograph of Phoebe Apperson Hearst.

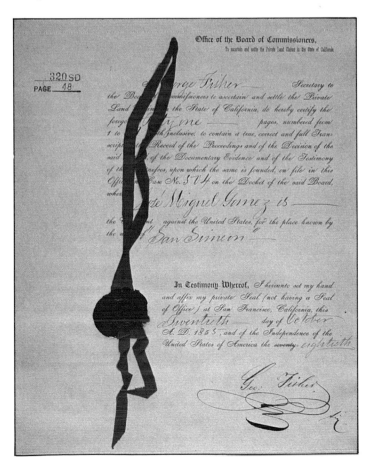

Verification of the Rancho San Simeon Land grant (on file in the Bancroft Library, Berkeley).

horses and dairy cattle.

In January of 1887, George Hearst was elected to the United States Senate by the California Legislature. Senator Hearst died from "a serious derangement of the bowels," according to the New York Times, on March 1, 1891, in Washington D.C. He left every penny of his $18,000,000 estate to his widow, Phoebe, who was at the time 48 years old.

On April 13, 1919, at the age of seventy-six, Phoebe Hearst died. She left the bulk of her $11,000,000 estate, including the land at San Simeon, to her son. Her parting marked a significant change in William Randolph Hearst's life.

Mr. Hearst was then fifty-five years old, an age when some men think of choosing comfortable shoes and easy chairs. William Randolph Hearst, too, retired in a sense. It was clear that despite drive, effort, and money, success in politics eluded him. World War I was drawing to a close. Perhaps all these events accidently coincided, but the fact remains that during the fall of 1919, W. R. Hearst found himself making his way to the Merchant's Exchange Building in San Francisco for an encounter with a woman named Julia Morgan, an architect. This occasion would prove to be the first step toward beginning work on the buildings at San Simeon. Between the two World Wars much of the enthusiasm, drive, effort, and love which he had previously given to politics, travel, and his mother were now poured into a new dream.

A masterpiece of romantic design, La Casa Grande soars cathedral-like from its hilltop setting.

Chapter Three

THE MAN, HIS ARCHITECT AND HIS CASTLE

". . . Miss Morgan, we are tired of camping out in the open at the ranch in San Simeon and I would like to build a little something . . ."

The Man

The fragment of conversation displayed above is part of a discussion which took place on the thirteenth floor of the Merchant's Exchange Building in San Francisco in 1919. The speaker, William Randolph Hearst, was talking to Julia Morgan, the family architect. Both were about to embark on a building project which spanned a quarter of a century.

When he was ten his mother took "Willie" on an extended tour of Europe for a year and a half. With her guidance, he toured art galleries, museums and historic monuments. During this first trip to Europe he embarked on his lifelong passion for collecting.

In the fall of 1882, he went to Harvard University. Harvard took itself seriously and was not prepared for William Randolph Hearst.

He did, however, develop a taste for the news media through his association with the "Harvard Lampoon." A persistent enjoyment of practical jokes eventually reached such proportions, as for example in celebrating the victory of Grover Cleveland over James G. Blaine, that Harvard suspended him short of his junior year.*

*There appear to be several versions of Mr. Hearst's expulsion from Harvard. Compare this version with W. A. Swanberg's in *Citizen Hearst*, page 39 of the paperback edition.

Possibly the first sketch for the Enchanted Hill by Miss Morgan. The note in Miss Morgan's hand refers to the "Ronda" motif of the single tower and facade of La Casa Grande.

The commanding view of the Hearst spread is from the air. The outdoor pool is in the background and Casa del Sol is in the foreground.

In 1891, Senator George Hearst died in Washington, leaving his entire fortune to his wife, Phoebe. At the time of his death his son had already revived the moribund *San Francisco Examiner* through a combination of publicity and innovative journalistic techniques, and he had made himself and his paper famous. Looking for new worlds to conquer, he gained a foothold in the New York publishing field, purchased the New York *Morning Journal*. Although the *Journal* was at that time a weak newspaper, Hearst thereby established himself in New York. Phoebe, with some reluctance, financed the venture by selling her seven-sixteenths interest in the Anaconda Copper Mining Company for $7,500,000. The *Morning Journal* became the flagship of the Hearst Fleet. The expansion of his publishing empire into New York was only part of a larger master plan. Hearst walked straight into the center of New York City politics and in 1908 was elected to the House of Representatives, his only real political success. It has been suggested that building the Castle at San Simeon grew out of his political frustrations.

In 1924, Alfred E. Smith won the Governorship of New York by 257,000 votes, defeating the Hearst-backed Republican, Ogden Mills.

Mr. Hearst's political failures did not diminish his thirst for real estate acquisition and building. The construction of the Hacienda at Jolon (1930); the new work at Wyntoon in Shasta County on the McCloud River (1930); the Florenz Ziegfield, the largest theater in the United States (1925); the Warrick Hotel in New York (1925); and the Santa Monica Beach House (110 rooms and fifty-five bathrooms), cost an estimated $1,000,000. After the purchase of the medieval castle of St. Donat, a fortune was poured into improvements, such as the addition of a swimming pool, three tennis courts, and a banquet hall. Mr. Hearst went on to purchase whole sections of Hamilton Palace in Scotland, which was sagging because of underground coal mining tunnels. He later built a fourteen-room bungalow in the Metro Goldwyn Mayer lot for Marion Davies.

These purchases and building projects consumed much time and attention, but San Simeon was always his favorite project.

His Architect: Julia Morgan

Julia Morgan had come to the attention of the Hearst family when she was working on the Hearst Mining Building at the University of California at Berkeley.

Julia Morgan was born in San Francisco on January 26, 1872. As a child, Julia was small and frail. In the fall of 1890, at the age of 18, Julia enrolled in the University of California at Berkeley, one of about two dozen coeds in a previously all male school. In her sophomore year Miss Morgan decided to become an architect.

After graduation in 1894, Bernard Maybeck encouraged her

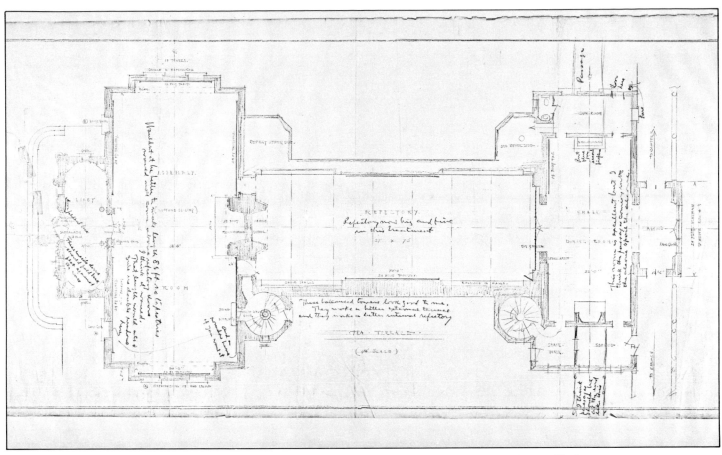

An early Julia Morgan sketch. The handwritten notations are those of Mr. Hearst informing Julia Morgan to extend one wall in the Assembly Room thirteen feet to accommodate one of his many tapestries.

One of thirty-three fully grown Italian cypress trees transplanted from Paso Robles to the Enchanted Hill.

to go to Paris to study at L'École des Beaux-Arts, the most prestigious architectural school of the time. What he failed to mention was that the Beaux-Arts did not, in fact, admit female students, and particularly foreign female students. In 1898, after much persistence on her part and with the help of Maybeck and others, she was finally admitted as the institution's first female student.

Julia returned to the United States in late 1901 or early 1902, at the age of thirty, with a degree in architecture. Shortly thereafter she won a job working with John Galen Howard. Mr. Howard was directing the designing of several of the buildings financed by Phoebe Hearst for the university campus at Berkeley. Julia also worked with Bernard Maybeck on a large vacation home for the Hearst family, Wyntoon, to be located on the McCloud River.

In addition, Phoebe Hearst asked Miss Morgan to remodel the Hacienda in Pleasanton. It was here in 1902 that Miss Morgan met William Randolph Hearst. Julia found her client's son knowledgeable about architecture.

She was a hard worker, a highly competent, if not brilliant, designer. During her life she was responsible for possibly over 800 buildings, which is a huge body of work for an individual practitioner.

La Casa del Monte's sun-drenched south court. "Mercury Resting" at left.

His Castle

Drawings for "A" house or the Casa del Mar were started immediately in 1919. In 1920 drawings were prepared for "B" house or the Casa del Monte, and the following year for "C" house or the Casa del Sol.

While working on the drawings for the first Guest House, Julia Morgan, giving rise to a flight of fancy, drew a tree-covered hilltop with three Guest Houses below, and a single tower rising above the billowing treetops against the sky. With variations the drawing was revised a number of times. One of the simple sketches captured Mr. Hearst's imagination. Julia Morgan evidently realized a fatal "error" had been made. But it was too late. The twin tower idea was suitable for a cathedral or monastery, but it in no way suggested a country villa which, after all, was the intended use of the building. This supposition is borne out by the presence in drawing collections of numerous sketches attempting to reconcile the cathedral "look" with the residence "function." All to no avail. The finished facade of the Castle holds closely to the first sketch.

All the structures on the hill were made of reinforced concrete which was an unusual construction technique at the time, and covered with exterior cement, plaster, stone, tile, or nothing, depending on the particular location.

Mr. Hearst maintained one of the largest zoos in private hands. He insisted that his animals be well cared for and visible.

The original Wyntoon located on the McCloud River. It was designed by Bernard Maybeck and Julia Morgan for Phoebe Hearst in 1902.

Such grading as was needed was accomplished by a steam shovel which was used jointly by the crews working in the gardens and the buildings.

Work continued on the Castle buildings from the early 1920s until 1937 when financial problems overtook the entire Hearst organization.

The projects which were never erected include a grand staircase connecting the drive to the upper terrace on the north, a ballroom over the water tanks on the far hill to the south, and a possible cloister or ballroom at the east end between the projecting arms.

The construction of the Castle differed from accepted practice in that the entire project was not conceived in advance either by architect Julia Morgan or client-architect William Randolph Hearst. Besides satisfying such necessities as sanitation, eating, sleeping, and social activities, and balancing such natural forces as gravity, orientation, wind, rain, and earthquakes, the spaces generated had to fit large-scale art objects, such as fireplaces, ceilings, tapestries, rugs, and wall paneling in the form of choir stalls, which Mr. Hearst had acquired and held in storage.

It is certainly clear that at times the built-in art objects determined the design of the building.

According to Ken Murray, in his book *Golden Days of San Simeon,* Miss Morgan said, "Mr. Hearst and I are fellow architects. San Simeon *is* Mr. Hearst."

To accommodate construction of the Castle, several mature oak trees were moved to other locations on the grounds rather than cut down.

The Neptune Pool; looking through the north colonnade to the ancient Roman temple and south colonnade beyond.

Chapter Four

THE POOLS, THE GARDENS
AND THE OUTDOOR SCULPTURE

Mr. Hearst had a large front yard. The Castle is five miles away from the Pacific Ocean and 1600 feet above it. His back yard was even larger. It consisted of 75,000 acres, slightly more than the original three Mexican Land Grants which constituted his father's original holdings.

As if the natural beauty of the place—the sea, the mountains, and the sun, embellished by natural flora and fauna—were not enough, Mr. Hearst added both animals and plants of his own choosing. The animals on the hilltop included an elephant, tigers, water buffaloes, yak, ostriches, and chimpanzees. He was always kind to the animals and wanted them visible to the guests.

Mr. Hearst raised Arabian horses and dachshunds. About seventy to eighty long- and short-haired dachshunds and Kerry Blue terriers were kenneled behind La Casa Grande.

The natural hillsides around the Castle were almost treeless. California liveoak (Quercus agrifolia) grew on the ridges. There were five other varieties of oaks growing in the arroyos and valleys. Mr. Hearst did not care for the bare ridges and hilltops and some twenty-four varieties of conifers were planted in the vicinity of the Castle. These included cypress, cedar, spruce, pine, yew, redwood, and giant sequoia. In many places the earth on the hilltop was too hard for manual digging and thousands of dynamite charges were used to create the basins for the trees.

Some trees were brought in full grown. For example, thirty-

Paul Manaut's "La Source," a sculpture group in the Moderne style of the 1920s.

Poetry in marble; the ''Three Graces'' — ''Brilliance,'' ''Joy,'' and ''Bloom '' by Boyer after Antoñio Canova.

because a master plan emerged after the fact as the work progressed.

Moving north or west to the Neptune Pool area, depending on the tour, we encounter one of the most beautiful outdoor spaces on the hill.

On the northwest side of the pool is a fragment of a Roman temple with the triangular pediment containing a Renaissance sculpture. The sculpture group includes Neptune, minus his trident, and two nereids. In fact, the whole temple fragment appears to be an assemblage of parts from different locations, but the detail of the carving is very well done and has the appearance of an authentic Roman fragment.

The south side of the pool contains numerous sculptured mermaids and mermen swimming in the water, and swans with cupids and/or putti on their backs. A basin of water at the next level contains a statue of the "Birth of Venus," the goddess of love, born from the sea foam. The seven carved Carrara marble statuary groups around the pool and in the alcove are by the French sculptor, Charles Cassou. Most are dated 1929 and 1930, and were done in Paris.

The semicircular colonnades at either end of the Neptune Pool were designed by Julia Morgan. The colonnades are made of white marble quarried in Vermont and assembled on the hilltop site. The four rectangular reliefs mounted on the walls of the colonnade are probably sixteenth or seventeenth century Italian bas-reliefs showing poets and philosophers of the classical world.

The pool terrace occupies a stunning location. The south end commands a view of the coastline in a great sweeping arc, while from the north the tops of trees in the foreground lead the eye to the distant hills, still part of the ranch. The semicircular colonnades at either end enclose the space without confining the viewer.

The pool itself is one hundred and four feet long, with a graduated depth of three feet six inches to ten feet. The pool has a capacity of 345,000 gallons. The bottom and sides of the pool are faced with white Vermont marble with a grid design made of a dark green marble called Verde Antique. Around the pool are lamp standards made of cast concrete in the shops on the hilltop.

A statuary group of three young women is the only nonclassical grouping, either in form or content, near the Neptune Pool. What appears to be a 1920s starlet is sunning herself on top of the wall.

The stairs leading to the next level are bordered by star jasmine, azaleas, and camellias. Twin sets of stairways rise from the pool level above the fountain to a semicircular ring of dressing rooms built into the hill. Above the dressing rooms is the Neptune Terrace surrounded by beautiful trees and shrubs. The planted area between the Neptune Terrace and the pool contains the various cypresses brought full grown from Paso Robles and beautifully maintained by the State.

The next level up from the Neptune Pool and just below the

The Indoor Swimming Pool as viewed from the diving balcony.

The Indoor Pool; "Abundantia."

Lucca, Italy. The statue in the pool is the nymph, "Galatea," by the Italian sculptor, Ansiglioni.

The Indoor Swimming Pool, to the rear of La Casa Grande, seems to have had an uncertain fate. One end is buried in the ground and the roof is flat to provide space for the tennis courts. The concrete arches were, no doubt, intended to be faced with stone. The roof tennis courts are on a level with the Esplanade and the azalea walk while the lower floor opens directly on the rear driveway for no apparent reason. The interior was lavishly decorated with Venetian mosaic of rich blue color laced with gold. Large scale marble statues are placed around the pool in an arbitrary fashion. One is left with the impression that early enthusiasm waned and the enterprise languished for lack of attention. The pool is known as the Roman Pool, but the structure has no counterpart in Roman antiquity.

The interior is now far more interesting than a few years ago. A large skylight between the tennis courts has been opened allowing light to penetrate the leg of the "T"-shaped pool, making it a sparkling blue grotto.

The main section of the pool is eighty-one feet by thirty-one feet and ten feet in depth. The pool has a flat bottom and the apparent curvature we see is an optical illusion. The leg section of the "T" is a four-foot-deep wading pool. The complex took three years to construct, and remains unfinished.

The 205,000 gallons of water reflect gold tile. The tiles were

Reproduction of "Apoxyomenos."

The sumptuous alcove of the Indoor Swimming Pool is home to "Abundantia," a seventeenth century Italian statue. The cantilevered structure above the alcove is a diving balcony.

A French Gothic mantelpiece, Tuscan Gothic lanterns, Spanish choir stalls, Sienese festival banners, Italian refectory tables, Flemish Gothic tapestries — and a king's ransom in fine silver make the Refectory the most impressive of San Simeon's rooms for many visitors. William Randolph Hearst, Marion Davies, and a veritable Who's Who of 1920s and 30s luminaries dined in this elegant room.

The Assembly Room's Great Barney Mantel from the Chateau des Jours, France. The name comes from Charles T. Barney, the New York tycoon, in whose Park Avenue mansion this stately piece was installed at the turn of the century. Following Barney's death, the mantel found a new home at San Simeon.

Moldings, balustrades, and other architectural details in cast stone — all San Simeon made in the Twenties.

A symphony of stone arches and windows on the rear elevation of La Casa Grande.

stretching out in front of the viewer, would be encountered. It is therefore a real shock to find the opposite, a great hall stretching laterally under the towers. Each tower is made of heavy solid concrete, contains sets of heavy bells, and holds a 2,500 gallon water storage tank for the entire complex. The structure of the room is taken for granted. Yet it is so vast, roughly eighty-three feet by thirty-one feet, that the proportions approach those of a dirigible hangar.

Two other elements will strike an architect on entering. First, in this huge room, there are only two windows, one at each end, placed so low that they seem to have slipped down to the floor. The choir stalls prevent them from being down too low and the tapestries prevent them from being up too high. We must remember that the entire room was designed around specific art objects.

The two different sets of choir stalls are Italian walnut and are used as paneling around the lower half of the Assembly Room. The massive room is a veritable storehouse of treasures. The size and complexity of it have the effect of overpowering the visitor. A pair of secret panels on either side open to provide access to the room exactly opposite — the Refectory.

The Refectory is the antithesis of the Assembly Room, in both style and layout. It is Gothic in feeling, rather than Renaissance. Upon entering one looks the length of the room as in a church nave. The windows are high near the ceiling, as op-

The Doge's Palace in Venice, Italy.

posed to low near the floor as in the Assembly Room. The room also appears to be sealed off from the next major room by a gold-plated wrought iron grill.

The 67 by 28-foot Refectory has a most unusual wood ceiling, presumably from central Italy. Just below the wood ceiling hang banners from Siena suspended perpendicular to the wall in an effective manner. Of all the rooms in La Casa Grande, this is the most pure in style and the least eclectic. The inspiration is nearly all Gothic.

The next room the visitor enters is the Morning Room. While not particularly important architecturally, it has some special features. After passing through the gold-plated iron grill, the visitor passes under an easily unnoticed but extremely beautiful arch. It is made of red Pyrenees marble, is from the Cathedral of Urgel, and is one of the many fine architectural components which Mr. Hearst collected. It appears to be Romanesque on the sides and Gothic on the top. Miss Morgan utilized such pieces with a great sensitivity and a definitive artistic eye.

Across the room from the entry is a vestibule which leads to the back patio. Before we go on to the technicalities of the construction, there are two suites of rooms which are seen on tours and which need to be examined for their architectural features: the Lower South Duplex and the Celestial Suite.

The Lower South Duplex is a suite consisting of an upper balconied bedroom cantilevered over a sitting room. The con-

A Venetian loggia reminiscent of the Doge's Palace facade decorates the exterior of the Doge's Suite in La Casa Grande.

The Roman god Neptune stands in the pediment of an ancient Italian temple; the swimming pool below is named after him.

Wearing a bodice of acanthus leaves and a Spanish-style corbel for a hat, a plaster of Paris caryatid stands Amazon-like in San Simeon's fifty-seat Theater.

Chapter Six

THE COLLECTION

Comparing the Hearst Collection to others has limited meaning. In the range and breadth of its categories it is unique. W. A. Swanberg states that Mr. Hearst ". . . became known to dealers in Europe and America as the world's premier push-over. It was understood everywhere that he could not take a normal view toward art, could not appraise a piece according to its cold market value, set a top price and stick to it . . ." Mr. Hearst appears to have started his collecting in 1898 and he continued acquiring until the mid-1930s. The value of the Collection lies not in the intrinsic worth of the holdings, but in the selection process by which they came to coexist. The apparent diversity has a unity which centers on Mr. Hearst himself.

Because the Collection and the art objects in it have an in-trinsic meaning independent of their location and another meaning in terms of their environment and proximity to other objects, we will examine them in two ways. First, we will see them in terms of their position in the Castle and then on a thematic basis in groups.

The Main Vestibule

Most people enter the Castle proper or La Casa Grande by the Vestibule which is extremely narrow and excessively high. The Roman mosaic floor cannot be fully appreciated as it is partly covered with tour mats. Uncovered portions should be examined as closely as time permits. The Vestibule marble mo-

Second Empire bronze group representing "Minerva" by Emmanuel Fremiet (Library).

The south alcove of the Library. The Greek vases on the plate rail above the bookshelves are but a fraction of the great number in the collection. The coffered ceiling is Spanish of the sixteenth century.

saic is circa first century B.C. The center section, which is the visible part, is entitled "Merman and Fishes."

Looking to the right and then to the left we see, respectively, two marble statues. The statues are backed by two tapestries, one of which is from Phoebe Apperson Hearst's collection. The statue to the right appears to be a rather silly woman seemingly cavorting around. She is called "Enchante" and she was made by the American sculptor Frederick Macmonnies in 1914. The original was done in bronze and is in the Metropolitan Museum in New York. The lady is balanced on one foot and gives the viewer the impression that she is inebriated. She appears to be at odds with the rather scenic environment. Behind her hangs an armorial tapestry dated 1684 and done for the Spanish Ayala family, after drawings by David Teniers.

To the left we encounter a Carrara marble statue group on the familiar theme of "Pygmalion and Galatea" by Jean Léon Gérôme, a nineteenth-century French sculptor. On the wall behind the statue hangs a Gobelin tapestry from the Phoebe Hearst Collection. Several sets of the design by Lebrun were woven when he was at the Gobelin factory in France. The set is entitled "History of Alexander."

The Assembly Room

The Assembly Room overwhelms the first-time visitor. It presents an almost insurmountable problem: What to look at? If you look straight ahead to the center of the room you will see a beautiful rock crystal presentation case and reclining Italian bronze figures of "River Gods" by Niccolo Pericoli (1500-1565) on a shining sixteenth-century Italian walnut table. Directly beyond the table is a rather imposing fireplace.

To the visitor's left is the north end of the room, with its bronze figure "Nymph Drinking" by V. Seifert on the center of the table. In the corners are a statue of Venus by Antonio Canova and a fragmentary torso of another Venus. Presumably this marble is a genuine antique from the time of the Roman Empire. If this is true, it is the oldest object in the room.

Glancing to the south end of the room one sees a large opened parchment book. The Gregorian chant book was hand lettered in 1826. The book is bound in leather and measures about thirty by twenty-four inches. Also at this end of the room and close to the path of the tour mat stands the bronze figure "The Setting Sun" by Adolf A. Weinemann, an American sculptor (1914).

The Theater

The Theater, illustrated at the beginning of this chapter, does not contain any art objects but the entire room is in itself a "work of art." Fourteen huge, grotesque, humanoid female figures are seemingly pinned to the walls. They are executed in the style of the late 1920s.

In the corner of the Billiard Room stands an Atwater Kent radio in 1920s Gothic style.

Harlequin lamp in the Art Deco style of the 1920s (Billiard Room).

Rare Urbino majolica inkstand of the sixteenth century. The original user of the piece provided St. George with a dragon-slaying spear in the form of a writing implement (Doge's Sitting Room).

Grandest by far of San Simeon's numerous guest quarters is the Doge's Suite in La Casa Grande. Silk damask wall hangings and mostly Italian furnishing and decorations convey the atmosphere of a sixteenth century Renaissance palazzo.

"Portrait of Alvisius Vendramin" by Jacopo Tintoretto (Doge's Sitting Room).

The Billiard Room

After entering the Billiard Room the visitor is aware of being confronted by the stone wall at the far end of the room. There is a strange combination of a round arched doorway, representing Romanesque architecture, placed under fine Gothic decorative carving. The semispherical triangles incongruously formed at the sides of this wall are surfaced with one hundred Persian tiles presumably dating to the seventeenth century. The west wall is occupied by a justly famous late medieval French tapestry.

The "Mille Fleur" or thousand flower design tapestry is about 500 years old. The work depicts a hunting scene and deserves close scrutiny for both form and content. On the right immediately upon entering is a small table lamp, less than twenty-three inches high. The figure which forms the body of the lamp is a harlequin with red shoes and a stiff cape in a kind of Batman costume.

The rooms on the upper level are so numerous and rich in content that we now become highly selective in our choices for discussion. None of the items mentioned should be missed, if at all possible.

A 1930s craftsman-made ceiling of plaster, wood, and paint and gilt decoration (Celestial Suite).

One of several larger-than-life-sized figures — in this case a representation of St. Petronius — in the Refectory's gigantic ceiling.

The Doge's Suite

The visitor on Tour Two is taken directly to the Doge's Suite after viewing the Neptune Pool and North Terrace. The room takes its name from the screen or grilles at the outer edge of the balcony, but contains no Venetian works of art except for a painting which Fredericksen attributes to the school of Tintoretto. "The artist, who was once thought to be Tintoretto himself, was one of Tintoretto's many followers. Bought from the dealer Goldschmidt in 1935." All of the windows of the suite look to the back courtyard and garden area and out to the Santa Lucia Mountains.

Each of the bedrooms of this suite contains excellent art objects. The north bedroom, which is seen first, contains an eighteenth-century Italian ceiling, a seventeenth-century carved walnut bed, and some excellent silver repoussé sconces. A large Italian needlework table cover of the seventeenth century hangs on one of the walls of this room. Also to be seen is a pair of unusual Italian Renaissance lapis lazuli lamps and, on the chest of drawers in the corner, a pair of exquisite green jade lamps in the shape of the phoenix.

The Doge's Sitting Room walls are draped with heavy blue decorative wall hangings making a rich backdrop for the multitude of objects found here. The ceiling, according to Fredericksen, a curator at the J. Paul Getty Museum, is one of only a few of its kind known to exist. The center portion was possibly

An ingenious combination of two French paintings, a set of Spanish armorial tondos, fragments of a Venetian cornice, and 1930s plaster and woodwork in the ceiling of the Lower South Duplex.

Apulian volute-handled krater — fourth century B.C. (Library).

Grecian askos of the fifth century B.C. (Library).

Eighteenth century majolica pitcher converted to an electric lamp (New Wing).

painted in the late seventeenth century from the school of the Flemish artist Joachim Wtewael.

The Library

The Library, directly over the Assembly Room, contains a wealth of books, over 4,500 volumes. All of the volumes were printed before the 1940s. Below the shelves are cupboards with a number of large bound volumes, most relating to fine art classification.

Within the Library is housed Mr. Hearst's entire collection of Greek vases casually displayed in a plate rail above the bookcases. Other objects of great interest, including part of the vase collection, are contained in lighted cases below the bookcase. This rare and outstanding collection of Greek vases will be examined in more detail later.

While still near the North alcove, the visitor should glance at the two pieces of sixteenth-century Italian furniture. The cap-inet-type table has an octagonal top and a rectangular base. The Savonarola folding chair is near the window.

In the South alcove we are drawn to a gilded bronze sculptural group, three horses pulling a chariot driven by a woman. Minerva, Goddess of Wisdom, is going out to do battle against ignorance and lust. The group is by a French artist of the nineteenth century, Emmanuel Fremiet.

"Madonna and Child and St. John" by Agostino di Duccio, a Florentine sculptor of the late 1400s (North Doge's Bedroom).

The Library Lobby contains a fine terra cotta bust of a Florentine nobleman. Those of us who frequent the Castle are often struck by his strange expression, a combination of wisdom, weariness, and wit. He seems poised, ready to speak out as he stares at us silently, his forehead wrinkled and his brow furrowed. One wonders if he has just finished a perplexing conversation in the 1920s-style phone which rests nearby.

The Gothic Suite

Immediately above the Library is the heart of the Castle. We are now on the third level above ground. The Gothic Study contains a wealth of really fine objects, some of which are very tiny, shown in glass lighted cases under the bookshelves. The other works of art are too numerous to be seen on tour. One must choose quickly between Persian jars, ivory tankards from Holland and Germany, a Russian tankard, a Sheffield silver wax jack, a Dutch silver drinking cup, and a pair of Venetian bronze lions. The top shelf on the bookcase supports a remarkable diversity of objects, among them a Venetian iron rooster flag holder, a number of Spanish reliquary busts, and a Spanish statue of St. Anne, Virgin and Child. Our advice is to bypass all this in favor of a handsome Gothic chimney piece with flanking Gothic doorways, a choice German clock from Augsberg, barely visible at the end of the room, and, especially, a pair of glass and metal lamps that are shaped like domed buildings

One of a pair of portraits by the Spanish court painter Bartolome Gonzales (Casa del Sol).

Unidentified portrait by the Dutch painter, Godfried Schalken (Casa del Monte).

"The Betrothal of St. Catherine" by an unknown Italian painter (New Wing).

which make for one of the truly unique possessions of the Collection.

The Gothic Study, like the Library, abounds with books on many subjects. The more than 7,500 volumes fall into four major classifications: history, biography, philosophy, and fine arts.

A visual tour of the room brings us to the focal point of the whole room, a portrait of a youthful Mr. Hearst painted by Orrin Peck, an early friend, the best man at his wedding, and beneficiary of his mother's assistance.

Beyond the Gothic Study facing the eastern mountains is Mr. Hearst's private office, the center of gravity of the whole hilltop complex. Because it is such a personal place, we feel the presence of this powerful, enigmatic man. His chair seems to be larger than most, maybe to accommodate his grander than six-foot frame. The backdrop of the mountains, as seen behind his chair, must have had an imposing effect on those commanded to appear there. At the present Mr. Hearst's private offices are not on any tour; perhaps that may change in time.

The Gothic Sitting Room, which both connects and separates Mr. Hearst's private bedroom from the North Gothic Bedroom, is packed with beautiful objects. Our interest in a beautiful chest covered with gold leaf is heightened when we learn that he kept his hats in it. The room contains about forty major items, too many to examine in detail on tour. Fifteen of these are statues from Spain, Italy, Alsace, France, Flanders, and Germany. Five of

the statues are of St. Barbara, either by coincidence or by design. To the left of the door leading to the north bedroom hangs a fine early Italian painting from Northern Italy. The painting is exceptionally large, of oil glazes on wood panels and is close enough to the viewer to be studied in detail. In the North Gothic Bedroom are two Spanish vargueños, a pair of Chinese carved rose quartz lamps, Austrian silver sconces, and a bronze bas-relief by Antonio Averlino, called "Il Filerate." He was one of the most important architects of the early Renaissance in Northern Italy.

The New Wing

The floor of rooms above the Theater is known as the New Wing because it was constructed later than the Castle proper. One has the feeling here that, although Mr. Hearst ordered the work done, he did not have the same interest in the result.

The Bathrooms

In some respects, the best examples of contemporary Art Deco style at the Castle are the bathrooms in the New Wing. If the designer (for Julia Morgan had assistance at this point), was hesitant in the treatment of the period rooms, he was truly at home in the bathrooms.

"The Venus of Canova" by the Neoclassic master Antonio Canova (Assembly Room).

A copy in bronze of Bernini's "Apollo and Daphne. (Doge's Sitting Room).

"Enchante" by the American sculptor Frederick Macmonnies (Main Vestibule).

The Kitchen

Returning to the first floor, we find the Kitchen. The rich metal surfaces are not aluminum, but a kind of stainless steel called "Monel Metal." Tile over the counters on the East wall carries the motto "Sine Ipso Fact V. Est Nihil" (Without Him There Is Nothing).

The pantry is twenty-four by fifty-one feet and the Kitchen is twenty-two feet eight inches, by thirty feet six inches. It contains an oil burning range, the baking ovens, four warming ovens, bread and roll warmer, steamer, steam pressure kettle, charcoal broiler, electric utensils and chopping block. The only apparent "art objects" are the curious brass birds that form the handles of the faucets.

The Groupings

Having discovered the diversity that exists in nearly every room, we are now ready to turn our attention to particular groupings within the Collection, independent of their individual locations.

As mentioned throughout the text, the ceilings are a special treasure of Hearst Castle. We recall no other museum or castle in the world where they are comparable.

As a group, the ceilings of the Castle proper and the Guest Houses constitute the most unique part of Mr. Hearst's Collec-

tion. The antique wood ceilings are suspended on wires from the concrete structure above. The ceilings of La Casa Grande are for the most part antiques from Spain or Italy, frequently pieced to fit the room. Most of the painted ceilings are from Spain, since the Spaniards excelled in this category of art.

The major lower floor ceilings, except for the Theater, are antiques from Spain containing elements of Moorish design. Moorish inspired wood ceilings are non-sculptural, involving intricate geometric decoration. When passing down the corridor leading from the Morning Room to the Billiard Room, the high corridor windows in the interior wall open to a wash room with a lovely ceiling in brilliant color and delicate scale. Mr. Hearst's private bedroom has a ceiling in the form of a truncated pyramid, certainly an outstanding example of early Spanish art of the fourteenth century. The ceiling contains fifty-three panels or coffers, each with painted figures of saints. The lighting here is only adequate, though sufficient to see the figures which should be studied in detail. The ceiling comes from the town of Teruel in the province of Aragon, Spain. Four other ceilings like it are known to exist. One is in Florence, two are in Spain, and the other is in Santa Barbara, California.

A ceiling of great delicacy and charm is in the Lower South Duplex. It includes oil paintings of "Endymion" and the "Departure of Phoebus" by the French painter, Simon Vouet, 1590–1649. Finishing off the ceiling are three pairs of armorial tondi from the Spanish Renaissance. The visitor is offered a unique

"The Engagement of Hasdrubal" is one of four monumental tapestries illustrating the "Deeds of Scipio Africanus," the Roman general who led his forces to victory over Hannibal and the Carthaginians in 202 B.C. (Assembly Room).

Fragment of a Graeco-Roman statue (Assembly Room).

opportunity to view this ceiling. When in the upper room of the Duplex, "Endymion" is directly over the bed. While in the lower level of the Duplex, the visitor should walk to the far wall and look up to see the entire ceiling.

The last ceiling selected for special mention is on the fourth floor of the New Wing. This room is a treasure house of art objects, but the ceiling is also surprisingly high. It is in the form of a truncated pyramid, and again the lighting is poor. In contrast to the one in Mr. Hearst's bedroom, the ceiling's pyramidal shape referred to as Moorish "Salamanca," extends very high in the air. This is truly a masterpiece and worth the whole tour to see.

Of all the precious furniture pieces in the Castle, the authors have chosen a few objects to suggest the richness of the whole. The jewel case at the North end of the Billiard Room is especially beautiful because of the pictorial enamel medallion set in ebony. The enamel work is from Limoges, France, and bears the date of 1562. Limoges artisans were famous throughout the Western world for their skill in developing decorative enamel work.

Chairs range from beautifully carved choir stalls, previously mentioned, to nondescript, overstuffed, formless seats that were typical of the period. The Assembly Room chairs were covered in a material especially made to match the frolicking children on the borders of the Giulio Romano tapestries. The covers were woven by Scalamandre's of New York in the late

The famous ''Cardinal Richelieu Bed'' in La Casa del Monte. The coat of arms in the headboard is of the Boffa family of Lombardy, Italy. Behind the bed hangs a Flemish armorial tapestry of the 1600s.

1940s. It is as interesting as it is unsuccessful, complicating an already complex area. There is no doubt that Mr. Hearst authorized this fabric cover himself.

There are various kinds of wooden chairs on the hilltop. Dante chairs are found in the Refectory. This set of forty-eight (twenty-two are on display) is of walnut, with seats and backs of leather covered with Italian velvet in a pomegranate design. This design is known as the ''Velvet of the Doges.''

An intricately decorated wooden chair can be seen in the New Wing, fourth floor (now in the last bedroom on the tour). It is a seventeenth or eighteenth-century Hispano-Moresque of X-frame construction, and is heavily decorated with certosina inlay work. Chairs with tapestry seats can also be seen. In room two of the third floor in the New Wing there are two tapestry covered armchairs called ''caquetoire.''

Several types of chests and trunks are to be found here also. These include marriage chests and leather or wood trunks. The marriage chests have hinged lids and are usually fitted on the inside. In the fourth bedroom of Casa Del Sol is a painted fifteenth-century Gothic marriage chest, with hinged lid and front. The interior is fitted with drawers and trays. Other pieces of furniture naturally include chests of drawers, beds, bedside tables, stools, prayer benches, cabinets, and framed mirrors.

The work of the Della Robbia family of Renaissance Italy is found in various locations in the Castle, but tends to be con-

Jewel cabinet with insets of Limoges medallions — French, 1562 (Billiard Room).

One of the most medieval, castle-like rooms is the Morning Room, just behind the Refectory and adjacent to the Kitchen and Pantry. The Gothic mantelpiece is from a French chateau.

centrated in the Della Robbia Room immediately above the Doge's Suite. On entering the room, pay particular attention to the small bust of a child. Portraying children as children in art was almost an invention of the Renaissance, and the first Renaissance building on the streets of Florence was the Foundling Hospital designed by Filippo Brunelleschi and graced by the famous circular medallions of full-figured children by Andrea Della Robbia. Here we can stand quite close to this object placed in the middle of the bureau. On the mantel is a relief of St. Joseph and child. Della Robbia is represented elsewhere as well, such as in the wreath found above the mantel in the Doge's Suite.

Roman sarcophagi made of limestone or marble grace the garden in various locations. Not all of them are seen on any one tour, and not all of them are authentic. Some are possible forgeries. Various styles of carving are illustrated, the most arresting examples in front of Casa del Monte, the "Nine Muses" are made of marble. Note the deep undercutting characteristic of late Roman work, as opposed to the shallow relief at the ends.

This is an excellent time to contrast classical with neoclassical work, for immediately above the sarcophagus is a statue of the "Three Graces" carved in the nineteenth century by Antonio Canova. One of the original prototypes of this statue is in the Hermitage Palace in Leningrad. The one at the Castle is a copy, probably by a French sculptor named Boyer, about

whom nothing else is known. In addition to the "Three Graces," one of Mr. Hearst's favorite statues, other neoclassical works include "Europa" by Fritz Behn, "Galatea" by Ansiglioni, "Pygmalion and Galatea," by Jean Léon Gérôme, and the Canova Venus in the Assembly Room. Bertol Thorvaldsen (1770–1844), a Danish sculptor who worked in Italy, is represented by a statue of Venus holding an apple.

Elsewhere in the Castle, the Lower South Duplex contains an exquisite statue of the Greek poet "Anacreon" with a lyre on his back. He is carrying a Bacchanalian putto and a cupid.

A large number of ceramic vases from ancient Greece, China, and Persia stand alone or have had their proportions ruined by the popular practice of wiring them for lamps, a vulgar idea still in practice today. The Greek vase collection has been subjected to closer scrutiny than any other group of objects in the Collection. After Mr. Hearst's death part of the collection was given to the Metropolitan Museum in New York. What remains is still one of the largest private holdings.

When viewing the Greek vases in the Library the visitor will not have enough time to see even a representative sample of all the types in the collection. There are a variety of shapes including the amphora, hydria, krater, pitho, rhyton, alabastron and askos.

The Persian pitcher found on the nightstand or bed table in Mr. Hearst's bedroom is strikingly contemporary due to the free flowing application of the glaze. The pitcher from Sul-

San Simeon's only example of genuinely Victorian art is this 1890s silver and enamel lamp by Tiffany & Co. It is believed to have been the property of Phoebe Apperson Hearst (Assembly Room).

tanabad, Persia, is from the twelfth century. A number of majolica ware pieces from Spain exist at the Castle, but none more beautiful than the lamp on the center table in the major top floor room of the New Wing. The New Wing also contains a unique Chinese jar from the Marion Davies collection.

The strength of the painting collection lies in its emphasis on Early Renaissance Italian work and in the personal subject matter of later work.

After Orrin Peck's portrait of Mr. Hearst, you should take the time to pay particular attention to the relief of Madonna, Child and St. John by Agostino di Duccio which hangs above the fireplace in the North bedroom of the Doge's Suite. Agostino Di Duccio was a major figure of the early Renaissance in central Italy. This soft polychromed work is beautiful and must be considered a work of major importance in the Collection.

The Castle contains numerous primitive Italian works done at a time when most paintings went unsigned. One of the most beautiful resides in the Assembly Room where it hangs near the Canova statue and cannot be seen on the present tour route. The painting is simply called "Madonna and Child with Angels" and is listed as fifteenth century.

The portrait of Bianca Capello, Dutchess of Medici, in the South bedroom of the Doge's Suite is by Angelo Allori, a mid sixteenth-century Florentine painter known as Il Bronzino.

The last painting is one of a pair of portraits. This one is by Bartolomeo Gonzales, a Spanish court painter of the sixteenth century. It is a portrait of L'infante Clara Isabella Eugenia, sister of Phillip III of Spain and daughter of the famous Phillip II. It hangs in Casa del Sol along with a matching painting of her brother. The historical value of the painting exceeds its value as a work of art.

The silver items on view at the Castle are probably only a small sample of a much larger collection. Much of the silver is found in the Refectory and is usually well explained on the tour. The Refectory alone contains an Irish mace from Dublin, a silver wine cistern of enormous size from England, candlesticks from France and Spain, a Spanish processional banner in silver, and an assortment of covered dishes from England and Ireland. Their location prevents close study but light from the high windows makes them shine on a bright day. The most visible item of silver is in the Assembly Room. A silver lamp, forty-four inches high, appears to hold the piano in place. Presumably it was previously owned by Phoebe Hearst, and was made for her by Tiffany & Co. in New York. The lamp has a silver shade with silver lace.

We have waited until the end to discuss the tapestries because not only are they superior in quality but, taken together, they constitute a wide diversity of styles and techniques. Space limitations in this book prevents a discussion and illustration of each important one, but we can at least alert you to those that appear significant.

Hispano-Moresque X-frame chair (New Wing).

Cupids and garlands add a whimsical note in slipcovered chairs and sofas (Assembly Room).

Terra cotta bust of a young boy. School of the Florentine master Andrea Della Robbia (Della Robbia Room).

The Assembly Room presents us with a wonderful opportunity to enjoy six large tapestries which contrast Mannerist and Baroque styles. The side walls are virtually covered with four matching great hangings designed by Giulio Romano, a sixteenth-century artist, in the Mannerist style. They formed part of a larger, ten-piece set and were completed around 1550. The set of ten weavings were in the French royal collection prior to the Revolution. We can only assume that the missing six panels have been lost to vandalism. French & Co. sold the four remaining panels to Mr. Hearst in 1921.

Contrast these tapestries with the circular flowing movement of the Baroque hangings on the end walls. The one at the North end, a single panel, is not to be overlooked. This Peter Paul Rubens design for an allegorical scene depicting the "Triumph of Christianity," as it is usually called, was woven in Brussels in 1625 or thereabout. It is reputed that the original Rubens cartoon for this weaving is in the Prado in Madrid; and it is furthermore assumed (only by some specialists) that the tapestry was part of the dowry of a certain Spanish princess, one Clara Isabella Eugenia, daughter of Phillip II of Spain.

The so-called "Daniel" pair of hangings in the Refectory is medieval in design with subtle color. They are Gothic in style and may well be the best tapestry set in the Castle. We will pass over the Morning Room tapestries, as they are of no great artistic merit, and go directly to the Billiard Room. The room is dominated by the stunning late Gothic or International

The stateliness of Renaissance art; a sixteenth century Italian credenza (Assembly Room).

"St. Joseph and the Child" flanked by angel candleholders — Della Robbia sculptures (Della Robbia Room).

Gothic tapestry of a hunting scene with horses, dogs, hunting trees, and flowers. Flowers are strewn on the ground or growing everywhere. This was a typical artistic convention of the late Gothic period. For this reason the tapestry became known as a "thousand flower" variety, although it would be better to refer to it simply as International Gothic. Notice the background figures are not smaller, but are placed higher in the composition. At the time this work was being finished, Italian painters like Massacio were already employing a new method of space representation called one point perspective. In terms of content, this hunting scene effectively depicts life in late medieval times. Two more Persian tile panels, using the Gothic method of two dimensional space representation, flank the French tapestry.

An ecclesiastical banner hangs above the nuptial bed in the north bedroom of the Doge's Suite and is of no special interest as to content; but the workmanship and needlework are exquisite and its inclusion here will serve as an example of the numerous ecclesiastical hangings throughout the Castle.

Room One of the fourth floor of the New Wing contains two remarkable tapestries. The main alcove, whose ceiling has already been described, has on the west wall a Royal Persian silk rug from Tabris, dated 1782. The hanging is rich in red and blue colors and is decorated with beautiful calligraphy in Pharsee, an ancient Persian language still in use today in some parts of the Middle East.

By contrast, the hanging in the Bedroom Alcove is a rare seventeenth-century Spanish tapestry decorated with a coat of arms. The chair at the foot of the bed is Florentine sixteenth century in a double "V" shape.

Most of the rooms in the Castle contain oriental rugs representing many famous rug-making areas of Turkey and Iran. Nearly all are partly covered with tour mats and furniture and are therefore difficult to appreciate. The rugs, tapestries, Greek vases, silver, and ceilings warrant special attention and monographs by specialists in the respective fields. The State of California should be urged to subject the Collection to careful curatorial scrutiny to enhance the benefit the public now receives.

At the far end of the Gothic Study hangs a compelling portrait of William Randolph Hearst painted by Orrin Peck in 1894.
Hearst was 31 at the time; the picture is of a quality reminiscent of the portraiture of John Singer Sargent.